EMPOWERED IN DESIRE

EMPOWERED IN DESIRE

ARIA NIGHTINGALE

CONTENTS

CHAPTER 1

Introduction

Welcome to Empowered in Desire: A Beginner's Guide to Sexual Dominance for Women. In this essay, you will learn a basic toolset you can start using right away to take your first steps. Although it covers the activity geared toward heterosexual male/female couples, the dynamics of exactly what is being explored here can be translated into any kind of relationship. I have stuck to a small, defined language to keep things simple so I can really drill it into you. At first, this was to help moderator operating systems mature from a script-file level toward a more complete and complex code, but now it remains by personal preference.

There are many people who consider the subject of sexual dominance or submission out of bounds. However, it is not necessary to have strong sadistic or masochistic cravings to be a "dominant" or "submissive". In every area of life besides sex, we accept that power is equally distributed among men and women. If the scarcity of experts in female-led relationships is any indication, many believe things should stay that way in the bedroom as well. But women can lead in most other aspects of life, why not in the bedroom? This is actually a question with many answers, but a significant part of the answer is that like you, many women do not know where to begin, and they face resistance from their partners who are also clueless. In this essay, I hope to not only give you a vision of what the life you desire would look like but also to show you what operates the mechanics of this world. By the end of it, you will have in your possession some of the code that operating systems of this world run on.

CHAPTER 2

Understanding Sexual Dominance

Sexual dominance is a way of "taking control" during a sexual situation. This occurs when one partner decides to take charge and direct his or her partner through a sexual act. You and your lover can switch these push-pull roles repeatedly. Sexual dominance is not the same as the role that we play in our lives. For example, if you direct a group of employees at work every day, you may not want to "take charge" and be in control in the bedroom. It is critical to understand that dominance and submission are not always determined by one's work life either.

The feelings surrounding a controlling partner vary depending on the individual. The act of a lover taking charge can be seen as anything from fun and exciting to demanding and overbearing. Some may feel that allowing oneself to act in dominant behavior means you could potentially lose control in other areas of life or feel guilty that they are too aggressive or unloving. Some may associate dominance with being male, and experiencing a submissive female comes off as destroying the feminist movement. And there are those females who are titillated by submission, where they experience their socially active position is suspended and they momentarily enjoy the sex roles that characterized the male/female relationships of the "good old days".

Defining Sexual Dominance

Within the overall context, the succinct definition of sexual dominance might stimulate an amorphous association of all types of visualized sexual behavior that increase frequencies of sexual activity involving the assumption of a dominant role. Therefore, dominance encompasses the role that one party plays in this process, while submission deals with the role of the other. However, neither is purely an action-based response required during sexual activity, as some individuals identify as dominant or submissive in seeking out sexual interactions, while others tend toward flexibility in their roles. Furthermore, not everyone who identifies as dominant or submissive is exclusively attracted to those who display markers of inferential submission or dominance. While negotiated power exchange forms a more extensive elaboration on dominance or submission because it involves a relationship and communication based upon larger attitudes or parts of a person's behavior, it remains a form of sexual dominance. This paper builds on this broader understanding as it explores the exchange of power during sexual encounters.

Some variation exists, however. Role-playing as submissive within BDSM activities hardly implies that the actor boasts reduced personal strength or is an inferior individual. Switching between the different roles of dominance or submission within the same character could occur, indicating that many individuals do not just perform a permanent role in their sexual acts, even if they often have a preference, and some others may use the act as a stimulus for pursuing infantilistic pleasure as a masked method to de-stress from a stress that is usually much worse beyond the game. Positions may vary in their level of active or passive for dominance or submission, but the act of dominance or submission is still present by encompassing the decision of the individual to play a specific role (whether socially constructed or not). In all cases, social psychological and other work on role-playing aid as an understanding for a focus on dominance in the sexual context.

Benefits of Embracing Sexual Dominance

While it's clear that there are many shifts, big and small, for a woman coming into her dominance, it's also clear that ultimately, it is an empowering force. It is an awakening that, in my own opinion, is due not to spanking someone, being whipped, or having someone kneel before you. No, these are the trappings of power. They are the markers for those outside of our lives. For us, power comes in having someone reveal their innermost secrets to us - responding to that. Power comes in having someone trust in us to keep safe the gentle essence of themselves. Ultimately, the empowerment that comes with embracing and embodying your sexual dominance is just another profound and touching part of you that seeks to make its way to the light of day.

Confidence and self-awareness are two important qualities that I think a lot of women will experience when they begin to embrace dominant desires. Women frequently report that as they become more comfortable with being in control of sexual activities, they become louder and more confident in their everyday life and are more assertive in asking for what they want in other areas of life. Some report that women who embrace sexual dominance are more in touch with who they truly are. They don't feel the need to impress anyone. Their own self-acceptance is what is important. This makes them very enigmatic and like a mystery, amongst other things. It is essential to listen to clues your body gives you as you explore dominance and submission, and to pay attention to how you feel inside when you're exploring.

CHAPTER 3

Exploring Power Dynamics

At the heart of sexual play is the interchange of giving and receiving power. Sexual dominance is simply about taking and possessing power, sexual submission is about surrendering and receiving it. The play itself is the magic interaction of that dynamic; the taking or surrendering of power becomes sexual stimulation. Many games come from this interchange of power and many expressions.

There are two basic types of power. Social Power is the ability to "make people do what you want" and Personal Power or self-assertion reflects "your ability to not let other people make you do what you don't want to do". These terms are often confused or used interchangeably. It is critical to explore the difference, as a woman on the path of dominance needs to possess a strong sense of Personal Power prior to developing her Social Power.

Negotiation and cooperation are needed to develop a dynamic of dominance/submission, to have someone submit one must be worthy. Part of your journey as you work to develop your Personal Power is to develop self-esteem that is rooted and unshakable. In this way, you awaken a sense of integrity and pride that will command the respect of others. Having this deep belief in yourself and your life will guide and direct your choices into the whole art of expression, whether emotional, intellectual, or sexual. Having Personal Power plays a huge role in setting the tone of what kind of power exchange you want within a sexual relationship. This is one of those areas where no chart, no handbook, and no rulebook can be written because it is your personal exploration.

Identifying your desires would be strongly suggested before trying to place a structure of any type of relationship or need based around it. Know what it is that you want to have in your relationship and what kind of sexual expression you are seeking. It is something that demands exploration of your desires. After having explored these concepts in yourself, you may find that forcing someone to submit to your will is not really what you want at all. The dominance you seek may be more of a nurturing, guidance, and control play scenario rather than a real pressing of wills. No matter what aspect you wish to incorporate, it must always and only be used safely and in a consensual fashion.

Types of Power Dynamics

As we begin our exploration of power dynamics, it is important to be able to categorize the different types as well as explain how these different types, in broad strokes, manifest within the realm of sexual dominance. In the purest sense, the power that we talk about in our sexual lives and in our relationships is not necessarily related to financial power, positional power, or political power. (However, these other sources of power can sometimes definitely establish an atmosphere of power or control, that in some measure can mirror those identified below.) In general, there is a pathology associated with strong men in BDSM communities. This pathology is fixed on playing a role and identifying dominants and submissives. However, it may be more accurate to identify specific relationships as those where power is a significant dynamic. In the discussions below, we refer to it as "topping from the bottom", not as a derogatory statement, but as a term generalizing the "essence" of the different types of power. There is nothing wrong with this type of relationship, unless both parties are pretending.

Within our relationships, we all seek different types of power relations. These different types of power are not at all exclusive. No relationship will exclusively fit into these categories. Sado-Material Power: "I control your immediate environment." Sado-Physical Power: "I have the physical power to enforce my rules and desires upon you." Natural power that comes from a placement: "Don't piss off the mistress of the house." Overt power that is established by an agreement: "Get away from it all. It is my realm. You will do as I say. Do we have a deal?" Equal power negotiated: In other words, we have equal price. I will trade what you want for what I want. Equal power trading: In other words, my assets are equal to your assets. Equal power trading: Your provision can earn your seat at the table.

Negotiating Consent

Aside from any social implications of power dynamics, a nonconsensual act is, by definition, an act of violence - thrusting it into the category of a crime rather than a social abnormality. In DV scenarios, fears of this variety of violence figure heavily and can interfere with one's natural desires. However, from the very first encounter you have with anyone of this inclination, start discussing it in terms of consensual encounters. The S/m communities are all the more vigilant about this because the nature of the activities you are discussing can seriously injure or kill someone. If you are discussing sexual violence occurring in a non-consensual context, it is clear that the Money Dominant is a psychopath. He can and should be faced with the full forces of the law. In both above-mentioned scenarios, remember to judge actions, not people. Just as the reader could have reservations about these services when they are couched in the guise of the victim's best interests, the statisticians and legislators creating the survey are likely to create questions reflecting their own judgments of desirability.

In the realm of consensual behavior, however, this above criticism loses legitimacy. Although we must question motives lying behind such research, assuming a significant portion of the population who experiment with D/s are mental patients stifles that same exploration, subtly denying the potential validity of the idea. In a completely consensual dominant and submissive relationship, "slave" acts are still just acting. But if the two parties are striving to create the illusion of true bondage, a few crucible tests must occur. For instance, one party struggling against a player's magic effectively ruins all the magic. Instead of simply watching spontaneous changes in a plot unfold, a player must use planning skills to invoke the illusion of spontaneity while maintaining interested and effective conversation between parties. In addition, players should make an effort to construct different playable narrative scenarios instead of the "kill everything with magic" or "overthrow the government" campaigns.

CHAPTER 4

Communication and Boundaries

An essential component of a healthy relationship, including any relationship which involves the pursuit of dominance, is the willingness and ability to communicate. In order to construct a scene or course of action which will be enjoyable for all involved parties, one must be able to express one's desires and concerns. Now is the time for self-analysis. The word "boundaries" has been actively used in feminist circles for years, to discuss the no-go regions for the individuals who need to be set. In sex, however, all lines are to be clearly defined as well. This is never more important than when one decides to pursue an untraditional avenue. The person who allows themselves to be dominated must trust that the dominant will respect their boundaries; the dominant must trust that the sub will be open about their fears and limits.

To pursue intimacy and trust through dominance also means pursuing open communication and clearly defined boundaries. No two boundaries are alike. That which one person might love, another could hate. There are only two criteria for personal preferences: that they are honest, and that they do not encroach upon someone else. If one desires to try something in an attempt to stretch one's limits, it is not only acceptable but also useful to share this with one's dominant. A good fellow will consider your request compassionately and decide whether it is wise to grant it. A final point to consider about boundaries is that both parties involved have them, be they simple or esoteric. A good dominant will reveal these boundaries to his partner, and will respect his partner's in return.

Effective Communication Skills

Effective communication skills are key in all facets of sexual dominance. Properly communicating will breed a healthy attitude, safety levels, and intimacy. It will make both parties feel better physically and emotionally, as well as raise both parties' self-esteem. Non-verbal communication will rarely occur in the dominant-submissive relationship, and this will generally be ignored or not made public. The most crucial aspect of communicating is trusting and non-revealing, and this is the one that each and every dominant needs the most assistance to work through. They worry that by revealing themselves to anybody else, they will be weak, they will not be able to perform, and they will be disturbed by what they want.

In my experience with dominants, it is undoubtedly not uncommon for me to see ones that are in awe of their submissive and slaves and worry about what they think about them as they are so thrilled themselves. But by taking it head-on, we must get over it! The initial step of talking with others is one that also advances your communication techniques. As the dominant should lead with full awareness, in many cases, she is most likely the one inspired to support the submissive or slave. Proper communication breeds positive attitudes and greater attitudes like that. Open, respectful, and non-judgmental conversation is crucial to the general order of society. Without spoken communication, the dominant and submissive relationship is purely non-consensual. Basically, a lot of harm could result if any of the counterpart parties do not consent orally to everything.

Setting and Respecting Boundaries

Setting and respecting boundaries are the core components of every quality sexual relationship. This is congruent with the model of clear communication, involving everyone in the circle of consent. One helpful idea is to think of boundaries as a threshold between looking (fantasizing) and touching (acting). This idea is helpful in that it acknowledges that sometimes fantasies may be such that disclosing fears or phobias wouldn't necessarily be on the top of everyone's agenda. Clearly, it would be a good idea to disclose if your desires fall in those areas, but it won't always be in the best interest of every person to give their imaginary friends a rundown of all their deepest fears fantasy-play could possibly agitate.

Just as it is possible to have one's hard limits shifted in the direction of softer, it is also possible that the play may help a bottom face their fears and phobias, or realize that they had been afraid of nothing all along—that they were already tough enough to do it! Each individual plays differently so this too should be an individual decision. Further, just as play can lead to the adjustment of limits in the protective direction, it can also work the other way: lines can shift in the direction of getting a bit puritanical, a bit drama-bound. This is just another thing to be aware of and watch out for in the quest for a hearty, sincere consensus.

CHAPTER 5

Building Confidence as a Dominant

uilding confidence as a dominant person takes time and effort. Not only is there the emotionally vulnerable process of entering into dominance to deal with, you're also confronting a lot of internalized messages about how you are 'supposed' to be in bed, as a woman. You might have to do some work to overcome your hangups at potentially being involved in power exchange play. The U.S. has a puritanical background that causes many to shun "abnormal" sexual behaviors and desires. It's your task to overcome those voices and feel okay about your desires.

You have to work through these feelings through guided self-exploration and reflection. You need to reflect on your own understanding of consent and limits and be able to respect the choices of others. Only then can you learn the correct way to wield your own personal energy in domination, to be able to connect with your submissive's mind and body through your own confident self-awareness. There is a lot that conspires to undermine confidence. You have some learned behaviors and will have to confront them in order to become a good and healthy dominant. Some of the resistance you feel may be created by the expectation that you are supposed to fit some stereotype of what a dominant looks and acts like. This perceived expectation was created out of the exhortations of a stack of BDSM erotica that more resembles male masturbation than a respectful and fulfilling encounter between actual physical human beings.

Self-Exploration and Reflection

We are discussing this at length because building confidence and exploring your dominant side is a big part of becoming a stronger, deeper, and more self-aware version of yourself. This has to do with you, so before we move onto how you become the best dominant possible, you need to understand just how important you are and should be to your partner.

One of the most heavily emphasized perspectives on BDSM is that submission and dominance are rooted within the person's desires and require an understanding of the body's responses to your touch. However, this view requires you to have an understanding of your desires - an understanding that can only be achieved through self-exploration of both yourself and your partner, and active reflection in order to grow as a dominant. These subtopics go into this at length, but here is a quick summation of just why building the confidence to dominate requires so much focus solely on yourself. There are a few things you need to be comfortable with within yourself before you can become a stronger, more confident, and sensuous dominant. The ability to be comfortable with your desires is an important advantage and has been reinforced by the literature.

Overcoming Insecurities

The thought of dominance can be equated to the idea of confidence that is commonly seen in the business world. Confidence, though partially inherent, is also something that can be put on, worn in order to overcome one's own insecurities. In D/s, dominance becomes a tool, toy or skill that can be learned to rise above a fear or uncertainty of our own. An intelligent and possibly more therapeutic approach should always come from seeking to overcome the insecurity. One popular method is by way of acting. As with other forms of therapy, the more you act confidently, the more you feel confident. Performing in the quality of a dominant may feel foreign, and undoubtedly awkward (at first), but 'faking it' can eventually lead to a real domination. That isn't to say that a woman should act through all feelings of feigned confidence. The dominating persona, or front, may be the first taste of dominance, but the imitation must end, must be outgrown, if the dominant seeks a true and fulfilling power exchange.

Innate worry, as viewed in this section, is far more problematic. The dominant female who takes position of her own deep desire will find a fear of loss. The character of a woman's dominant, however theatrical, is a character, and to make her more than a mere trick must be a woman who has overcome much of her own anxious hesitancies. While practicing dominance, it's not unusual to be hesitant, or to feel pressure or mistimed. There exist many male submissives who enjoy receiving a punishment eminently because they cannot achieve such a reward normally. If nothing else, such errant behavior is a calculated trapping of a man who will earn a punishment just to be dominated. This, too can feed oneself with the fine confidence thrown by one's own taking, punishment, power.

CHAPTER 6

Practical Techniques and Play

Physical Techniques: Hair-pulling, Pinching, Biting, Spanking, Stroking and Pain Play, Sensory Deprivation, Restraints, Playing with Exposure, The Pinch-n-pull, Psychological Techniques Definitions of Domination, Definition of Submission, Mental Turning Points, Control and Discipline, Playing with Fear, Playing with Embarrassment, Pride Play, Role-Playing and Fantasy Exploration Distinguishing Fantasy from Reality, There is a Difference between what you Do and Who you Are, Choosing a Persona, Deciding about Costuming, Time, Place, and Context, Playing with Gender, The nurse/male patient, The boss/secretary, The master or mistress/maidservant, The maiden/male rescuer, The amazon/male captive, Is It Right to Play Dominant Games?

This section will give concrete directions for how to carry out the specific kind of play that we've been discussing up to this point. They are guidelines, not prescriptions. Clarifications have been provided where such imagined guidance may prove unclear.

Technique #1: The Physical Technique. All sorts of sequences: pulling the hair and then pinching shoulders, biting an earlobe and then dominating a conversation, spanking sharply and relentlessly and then gently caressing the spot and starting to stroke—where? Whichever stroke matches your mood and your sense of your partner's potential. Psychological restraint begs for release (the physical), and the release excites because it has been earned. The wrinkling of cloth laid over wrists to be tied with a knotted bed-sheet should be heard in order to experience the sensation of power. If you are intrigued by this, stay tuned. In the section called "Special Considerations," we delve further into how this kind of approach does not preclude love or compassion.

While this way of sexual interaction may not appeal to everyone, it is peculiarly tailored to the nuances and gap between control and freedom that can exist within female desire. For those who are interested, however, the first step in the practice of this potentially rewarding, trusted, and caring cruelty is up to you. Read on—carefully!—for a deeper introduction to some of the techniques of sexual domination. Let your fear and trepidation dip into your desire rather than keeping them isolated from the way you interact with your lover.

Physical and Psychological Techniques

In any sex guide, the most fun part is the practical part, right? Be hard and get even harder. In physical approaches to practice, you can elicit physical signs of surrender or use bodily cues to manipulate the person you're playing with to do what you want. We then address psychological approaches to practice, in which you can use simple techniques to affect the state of mind and reduce resistance in the person you want to dominate.

In fact, this section is probably redundant; in practice, physical and psychological approaches blend and complement each other. Religious SM players will likely roll their eyes when they read this list, and we know why: Just like you, we bring wholeness to our play.

We want a bit of everything - softness to balance out softness, sweetness to balance out sweetness. We want our physicality to have an edge of dominance, and our dominance to have an edge of acquiescence. And we know that dominance and submission are not primarily about sex or bodies; they're about who decides, who takes the risks, and who bears the responsibilities. Remember that we take a more expansive view of play, and thus of practice. Most of the techniques in this section should only be undertaken if and when you trust your own intentions. Don't be scared by the barky parts of yourself! Be honest about them, and try to figure out what they need from other people in order to calm down. There's a certain pleasure, you may find, in discovering that you do not have to act like a character to enjoy a few sexual variations.

Role-Playing and Fantasy Exploration

Every one of us has indulged in the enchanting world of role-playing games and make believe. We know very well what it is to step into another character for an evening of fun. In a way, the BDSM world is sort of like that. You might take on the persona of a succubus or the Queen of Sheba for a short while and revel in the feeling and the power of that character. So, there is a way in which our desires can be played out and lived through in fantasy in a society that might frown upon us walking down the street with a cuffed sub in tow. Another point on role-playing and playacting is that our sense of play has almost always been private. We separate play from work, right? So why not take those similar steps between life and work and play? All three define us; we are dominants in our work, in our roles in our families, in our social groups, are we not?

Well, here is the kicker. Role-play is a large element of many relationships, BDSM or not. Imagine having children and running a household if all your parents ever saw you as is the dominatrix you really are. We would wind up sort of like smokers at a tobacco convention. You really don't want to be around people when that gets let out. So, the same goes for our sexual life with our partner. Some things do not mix well. You have to start slowly. Start on a level that will acquaint you with each other's ideas of comfort and credit. Once you establish the parameters of your fantasies, you can take them from there.

CHAPTER 7

Safety and Aftercare

Safety As much as sexual dominance is about making the desires of the dominant partner a priority, safety involves making sure the well-being of the submissive partner is a priority. Safety starts in your thinking. It is impossible to guarantee that sex is completely risk-free, physically or emotionally. It is your job as the dominant partner to do what you can to alleviate the risks. The safer you make the encounter, the more likely everyone is to keep their sanity. The first key to safety is always picking a partner or partners that you can place your trust in at a time when trust is much-needed. Do not play with anyone who uses scare tactics to get you to do something you do not feel okay with. Any time you feel little warning bells going off in your gut, it is okay to slow down and talk or stop altogether.

Aftercare Oftentimes, a submissive partner will bottom out into what's called "sub space" during an intense scene. It is an endorphin high that hits the submissive after the scene is over, and possibly hours after. Peace and serenity take over. Aftercare is the first large step in helping a submissive back from sub space. Keep lots of water on hand, and sometimes, juice (it aids in processing sugars more quickly). Keep plenty of soft pillows, blankets and towels to go around. It's gross and it happens, so when it comes – have supplies ready! Careful or overly warm submissive partners might suffer from heat rash and require a bit of cooling powder (do not pick any powder, and Gold Bond is a popular one to try).

Importance of Safety Measures

In all the real, practical talk of learning to give guidance and criticism, establish protocols and punish insubordination, the most important aspect of sexual dominance is often left out. Safety measures should be common sense, but, regrettably, often are not. I realize this book is aimed at beginners who don't know what kind of play they'd like to do, but if you're at a point where you're definitely considering erotic dominance and are actively reading up on it, this is the most important advice I can give you: follow all safety measures. They exist for a reason.

No advice given here or safety measure listed will be upheld as absolute within the larger BDSM community; they vary greatly among individuals. An extensive glossary of terms and conditions is offered here - if you consent to a dominance dynamic with someone, I will assume you're reading these entries and are familiar with each item. Your safety and the physical and emotional well-being of all participants in a relationship where some play the role of the dominant and others, the submissive, and negotiate accordingly with regards to protocol and punishment and the varied sexual exchange between dominant and submissive; between top and bottom within a given (meta) textuality; are expected to be your first concern. While relations of self and other vary in countless ways from one work to another, an allowance is offered to surface commonalities we believe will be repeatedly been redeemed in the conduct of BDSM relations.

Providing Aftercare Support

People engage in BDSM for many different reasons, all of which are valid. However, emotional exchanges are an essential part of doing scene work. It's important to care for both bodies and hearts as part of sexual dominance. During emotional aftercare time, the bottom may laugh, cry, and/or process emotions from the scene.

Someone new at sexual dominance, who doesn't feel like they need any aftercare, should still provide some to the bottom they partner with. This helps to build trust and establish the emotional connection needed for a scene to proceed. It shouldn't be a surprise that aftercare may last a few seconds, a few minutes, or an hour. The stronger the scene, the more aftercare is likely to be needed.

Types of aftercare in BDSM might include: - Physical: ice packs for bruises or overtaxed joints, looking for cuts - Emotional: Reassurance of love, admiration, appreciation; sometimes just talk again about the feelings after, check in about them. This should be led by the bottom—follow their cues. - Checking in: Make herself receptive to feelings after the emotions; non-judgmentally asking open-ended questions: How did it feel to you? Did that strike you as cathartic or heating or tender? If she asks yes/no questions, she's asking judgmental ones: was that powerful? Did you like this or that? This can upset the bottom, here, in the early stages. People are baffled to discover sadness and bleakness associated with pain, and in the bottom-darkness, hearing judgment makes it that much more difficult to reconnect. - Time: Give their top time because often the top will need attention more as the bottom processes and dances off the endorphin high of play.

CHAPTER 8

Navigating Stereotypes and Stigma

One of the struggles women face when they are beginning to explore sexual dominance is the gauntlet of stereotypes and stigma facing female dominance (let alone outsider sexualities like BDSM). This is a less tangible struggle because there may not be concrete answers regarding who is safe to talk to about dominance, when to be openly dominant, or whether to be "out" as a dominance at all, or only in some circles. However, it is important to lay the groundwork for you or to reveal and move with the day-to-day dance, night-to-night tension of making essentially performative choices under an oppressive eye that simply should not be, yet is. Furthermore, it is possible to internally work to heal from the deep wound of stigma, and to help educate us about the realities of what female sexual desires can look like. After all, consensual sexual dominance can be a beautiful, lucid expression of one roundabout of what is possible for a woman freed even a little from false fears, so why shouldn't it be known as such?

"Fear of either acting out of your norm, or fear of being discovered to not be the norm" is one definition of stigma. Society is invested in imagery rather than reality, and is a powerful force to perpetuate the idea of a singular, sexless white female norm, in ways incongruent with the sexual spectrum and history. As always, religion, state, medical professionals, society and its neat little diagrams may work to shame from the shadows, the pack-attacks, the safety-in-numbers entertainment of the barely aware, but the pale society image is, at the very least, ignorantly off-putting. When you happen to align directly with that image, you may still find yourself and your desires twisted through societal lens to take on an either/or meaning, and be sincere or distinguish between them to assert real contrast as one's true desires as separate from the performance. In that way, a non-official performance may turn into a play between social education, sexual healing, and ultimately fun—and can be an effective tool to garner attention for the reform on the teacher as a lover rather come across to say look at the freak go just to be frowned at.

CHAPTER 9

Empowering Others Through Dominance

The real element of empowerment for women in the expression of sexual dominance comes from two sources: 1) the acknowledgment and acceptance of one's nature, no matter what that nature may encompass, and 2) the understanding of the other side of being someone possessed of mainly submissive instincts. For the former, it can be devastating to feel that one is abnormal because society has set certain standards for behavior, and many women feel that way about their own sexual nature. That in itself is a cause of stress, which isn't helped by the general outlook of those defined as "normal" toward those not classified as such. Repressed sexuality is often a factor in the formation of acute mental illness and/or numerous tragic incidents, up to and including – in a few cases – murder or suicide. Dealing with the side that has been leveraged into non-mutual acceptance due to society's misunderstandings can help to offset or reduce some of those problems, leading to an increase in feelings of self-worth.

On the other hand, for those who aren't suppressed individuals feeling driven to the extremes mentioned above, sexual dominance offers women another, more tangibly realized, form of empowerment. Dominating others gives one a sense of control, which is often the opposite of the sort to which many of these women are subjected by society. In modern times, many women and men alike are seeking out avenues that will lead toward lives more in keeping with their personal aspirations. In these times of great societal upheavals, everyone is seeking out those particles of "good" that make life worth living. Among these, the question of equality of treatment has been addressed as justice for all. It is time for a more complete understanding of equality, in everyday relationships as well as those that endeavor to offer any and every possible advantage likened to the expression of life itself, and this is comparable in many separate areas.